Marriage and the Counsel of God

Workbook

Marriage and the Counsel of God

Workbook

MICHAEL A. ESCHELBACH

Wipf & Stock
PUBLISHERS
Eugene, Oregon

MARRIAGE AND THE COUNSEL OF GOD
WORKBOOK

ISBN 13: 978-1-55635-347-5

Manufactured in the U.S.A.

Contents

1

Introduction

THERE ARE as many reasons to pursue marriage counseling as there are people to seek it. But there are four directions from which forces compel us to counsel before pursuing a marriage or before seeking to terminate one: forces from above, beside, below, and within. First, the force from above is God. God created us to live in communion with Himself and each other. He defined that communion even more specifically by creating new life through the union of husband and wife. The wisdom of our creator is the first and most compelling force to seek the fulfillment that comes within a relationship that is lived according to His design.

Second, a good marriage is important to the community of people around us, near and far. The world itself, whole nations and small communities, is only able to recognize and devote significant effort toward noble causes when marriages and families are sound and vibrant. Christian congregations provide an environment of mutual support when marriages within it are healthy and encouraging. Extended families also benefit from the common effort to know the blessings of relationships according to God's design.

Third, a good marriage is essential to those below—the children. Children learn about their relationship to God by observing their fathers and mothers. The fallen human nature of children needs a united perspective and response from parents. The souls of children need the united yet multifaceted witness of parents.

Finally, each person involved in a relationship has a soul that yearns to know the union that God intended. The distorted thinking of human nature and the aggressive nature of perversion (especially through the media) make a life within God's Word and grace essential if goodness is to be discovered and protected. Our souls need truth to know what makes life and grace to inspire us to that life. Such absolute truth and grace can only be found in the Word of God.

God's Word as the only reliable response to human need in relationships is the origin of this book and the reason for its title, *Marriage and the Counsel of God*. What follows is the product of more than twenty-five years of study coupled with more than twenty years of marriage counseling (pre and post). The clarity of God's design for relationships as communicated in the Bible and fidelity to that provide the most reliable means of developing, sustaining, and restoring good marriages. The text generally follows Martin Luther's chief parts of the Christian faith from his Small Catechism: The Ten Commandments, The Creed, The Lord's Prayer, Baptism, Lord's Supper, and the Office of the Keys. However, longer sections of scripture are considered where appropriate and other matters of counseling are treated in supplementary sections. For example, the counseling proper begins with a careful treatment of Genesis 1–3 since that is the foundation and source of everything else the Bible has to say about marriage and relationships. Ephesians 5 is treated in greater detail under the second article of the Apostles' Creed because Christ provides the other great witness to God's intent for relationships.

This companion workbook should be given to each of the individuals seeking counseling. They are to complete the battery of questions (2.b.) before counseling begins and then continue to read ahead make notes on the subsequent materials. As the counselor leads the individual or couple through these materials the counselee(s) can refer to their notes for questions, disagreements, or interest in further discussion.

2

Preliminary Outline and Supplementary Materials

2.a. Preliminary Concerns—Outline

I. Preliminaries
  A. Consent of those responsible to God for your well-being
      1. Parents of the woman
      2. Parents of the man
      3. Pastor
  a. Eligibility in regard to the state
      i. Marriage license
      ii. STD counseling
  b. Eligibility in regard to family
  c. Eligibility in regard to the Church
      i. Of one faith
      ii. In the image of Christ and His Church
      iii. With obvious and consistent morality/virtue
  B. Proposal and acceptance
      1. With full capability to fulfill what is required
      2. With a full understanding of what is being proposed
      3. Freely and without deceit or duress

II. Preparations
  A. Counseling to insure all of the above
  B. Final consent of pastor
  C. Rehearsal . . . date/time_____
  D. Wedding arrangements in human modesty to the glory of God
      date/time_____
  1. Texts
      2. Music
      3. Apparel; marriage party (people); conduct before, during, and after
      4. Photography: before, during, after
      5. Reception
  E. Use of the church
      1. Pastor
      2. Organist

3. Musicians

4. Cleaning

III. Post wedding pattern of living
   A. Faithful involvement in the life of God's Church
   B. Personal devotions (pulse)
   C. Private confession and absolution (blood pressure)
   D. Faithfulness to vows—in every respect

2.b. Questions for Couples to Answer before Counseling

The purpose of these questions is to help you take time to consider the thoughts, attitudes, and characteristics you will bring to marriage. The better you know each other, the less chance there is for misunderstanding and the more appropriately you can implement God's counsel to you concerning marriage.

Please take your time to thoughtfully answer these questions. Each of you should answer these questions separately and in electronic form if possible. This will allow you to reconsider, edit, and revise your answers. This will also allow your counselor to import your answers into a table for comparison. We will refer to both as opportunity arises in the course of our counseling.

1. How much study/preparation do you think is necessary before planning to get married?
2. How much concentrated study/effort do you think is necessary after the wedding?
3. Why do you want to be married in a church?
4. What are the most important factors to you in planning your wedding (in order of priority)?

(Depending on your answers, you may wish to stop here)

5. How long have you known each other?
6. How well would you say you communicate with each other?
7. Why do you want to get married?
8. When did you become engaged?
9. Have you been engaged before?
   a. How long ago?
   b. What happened?
   c. Is this fully resolved?
10. Have you been married before?
    a. How long ago?
    b. For how long?
    c. What happened?
    d. Is this fully resolved?
11. Do you have any physical handicaps or disabilities that might affect your marriage and have you faced these to your mutual satisfaction?

12. Are you acquainted with the emotional characteristics of your intended spouse?
13. What concerns do you have/what changes would you like to see?
14. How do you feel about the social circles in which your intended spouse has lived?
15. How will your courtship contribute to your marriage?

1.1.1 What is your religious affiliation?
1.1.2 What is your intended spouse's religious affiliation?
1.1.3 What is the history and nature of your involvement in your church?
1.1.4 What are your thoughts regarding being of one faith with your spouse-to-be?
1.2.1 Can people have the same faith and belong to different churches? Explain.
1.2.2 What is / has been God's part in your relationship?
1.3.1 How are you observing the "Sabbath" in your relationship?
1.3.2 Worship life?
1.3.3 Bible studies?
1.3.4 Daily devotions / Bible reading?
1.4.1 How do your parents feel about this marriage?
1.4.2 Have you met with your parents to discuss the marriage?
1.4.3 Have your parents met with each other?
1.4.4 How do you think you will get along with your intended spouse's family?
1.5.1 Have you ever had a fight?
1.5.2 How often?
1.5.3 What are they about?
1.5.4 How do you resolve them?
1.6.1 Are you living together at this time?
1.6.2 Have you lived together in the past?
1.6.3 Are you / have you been sleeping together?
1.6.4 What is love?
1.6.5 How did you come to your views on love, romance, and marriage?
1.6.6 Do you plan to have children?
1.6.7 What have you determined about the place of children in your marriage?
1.6.8 What are your views on birth control?
1.7.1 What are your plans for career?
1.7.2 What priority will those plans have in your life?
1.8.1 Are your thoughts toward your intended spouse always positive?
1.8.2 When are they negative?
1.8.3 How do you deal with these thoughts?
1.9.1 Are you content with your life?
1.9.2 What changes would you like to make?
1.9.3 What part do you see your intended spouse playing in the life you would like to lead?

2.1.1 What part does God play in your physical life?
2.1.2 What part do you think God has played in your relationship?
2.1.3 What do you believe about the nature of "marriage"?

2.1.3.1 What is the essence of the relationship?

2.1.3.2 What is the purpose of the relationship?

2.1.3.3 What are the roles of each spouse?

2.1.3.4 How long does this relationship last?

2.1.4 How familiar are you with what the Bible says about marriage?

2.1.5 How do you plan to provide for your physical needs once you are married?

2.1.6 How do you plan to provide for your spiritual needs once you are married?

2.1.7 How will you handle the various responsibilities of maintaining a home?

2.1.8 Where do you plan to live after you are married?

2.1.9 What is your view on debt?

2.1.10 How does that compare to the view of your intended spouse?

2.2.1 How are you saved?

2.2.2 How does your understanding of salvation affect your relationship with your intended spouse?

2.2.3 How does/will your relationship bear witness to your faith?

2.3.1 Where does faith come from?

2.3.2 What part does faith play in your life?

3.0.1 How often do you pray?

3.0.2 What do you pray for?

3.0.3 What does it mean to pray to "OUR" Father?

3.1.1 What is God's name?

3.1.2 How will God's name be "set apart" in your marriage?

3.2.1 What is the "Kingdom of God"?

3.2.2 How will it come to your marriage?

3.2.3 How might His kingdom come to others through your marriage?

3.3.1 What is God's will for you as an individual?

3.3.2 What is God's will for you in relation to your intended spouse?

3.4.1 What is "daily bread"?

3.4.2 What are the most essential things for your life?

3.4.3 What do you think are the most essential things for the life of a marriage?

3.5.1 Do you distinguish between the kinds of things that people do wrong? How?

3.5.2 What is forgiveness?

3.5.3 What role do you play in forgiving others?

3.6.1 What temptations do you struggle with?

3.6.2 What temptations do you see in your intended spouse's life?

3.6.3 How do you / will you deal with temptations?

3.7.1 What kind of protection does God provide for your relationship?

3.7.2 How would you react if your intended spouse was seriously injured or killed before your marriage?

4.1.1 What is baptism?

4.1.2 How does baptism work, what does it do?

4.1.3 Who should be baptized?

4.1.4 What part, if any, does baptism play in your relationship?

5.1.1 What is "Holy Communion"?

5.1.2 Who should come to Communion?

5.1.3 Should anyone ever NOT come to Communion?

5.1.4 How is real Communion established and sustained?

5.1.5 What part will Communion play in your marriage?

6.1.1 What will you do if your marriage begins to go badly?

6.1.2 What is your thinking about divorce?

6.1.3 What do you think about separation?

7.1 What are the "vital signs" of marriage?

2.c. Flowchart of Preliminary Marriage Matters

2.c.i. Flowchart of Preliminary Marriage Matters – Outline

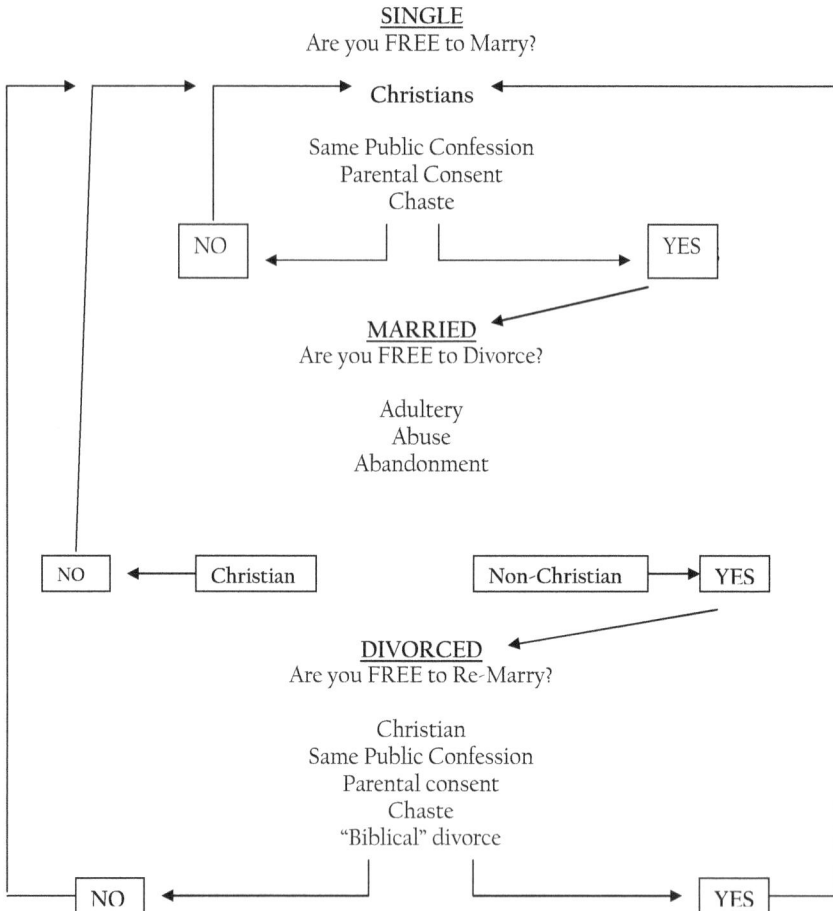

<u>SINGLE</u>
Are you FREE to Marry?

Christians

Same Public Confession
Parental Consent
Chaste

NO   YES

<u>MARRIED</u>
Are you FREE to Divorce?

Adultery
Abuse
Abandonment

NO   Christian   Non-Christian   YES

<u>DIVORCED</u>
Are you FREE to Re-Marry?

Christian
Same Public Confession
Parental consent
Chaste
"Biblical" divorce

NO   YES

2.d. Critical Diagnostic before Proceeding

I. John 6

"The Spirit is the life-maker; the flesh profits nothing. The words I have spoken to you are Spirit, and they are life."

God's Word helps, my thoughts/attitude harm.

A. Proverbs 3:5–7

" . . . Do not be wise in your own eyes . . ."

My understanding/lack of genuine understanding has affected my marriage negatively.

B. Proverbs 16:25

"There is a way that seems right to man . . ."

What I feel justified in thinking/saying/doing on my own behalf only makes things worse.

C. Isaiah 55:1–13

" . . . for my ways are not your ways . . ."

My ways are contrary to life and powerless to make things better; God's ways are always life-giving and provide the energy to affect what they describe/command.

3

Genesis
Model of Paradise Created and Destroyed

1 Corinthians 6:19

"Or do you not know that your body is the temple of the Holy Spirit who is in you . . . and you are not your own?"

A. Genesis 1:26–31

". . . in the image of God, . . . male and female, He created them . . ."

The image of God is the relationship intended between man and woman; man is responsible for, woman responsible to. (See 1 Corinthians 11:3)

" . . . let them have dominion . . ."

One purpose of man and woman in their relationship is to have dominion—to take care of the created world (NOT to alter, accumulate greedily, find discontentment with, etc.).

". . . God blessed them . . . 'Be fruitful and multiply . . .'"

Man and woman are to help God in His creative activity through the bearing and raising of children.

" . . . 'See I have given you every herb . . . and fruit for food . . .'"

In paradise there is no need for others to be sacrificed for me. Everyone and everything can fulfill its purpose for others and live.

B. Genesis 2:15–18

" . . . God took the man and put him in the garden to tend and keep it . . . "

Man alone, before there was woman, was given the responsibility to care for and tend the garden. This purpose and responsibility has not changed.

". . . but of the tree of knowledge . . . you shall not eat . . ."

Man was given a place to demonstrate his trust in God by diligence in his purpose and refusal to seek more knowledge than God had given.

God's choices for us are always good; ours are always bad for us and others.

Disobeying God's command meant rejecting His Word, losing His breath/Spirit, losing His life.

". . . It is not good for a man to be alone . . ."

As God the Father was not alone but begat the Son from eternity and as God was not alone but created man as an object of responsibility and care, so man was incomplete without an object of constant care and responsibility.

"I will make him a helper to remain before him. . . ."

Man was created to be fruitful/multiply and to care for creation. Woman was made to be cared for and help man fulfill his purpose. Perfection requires man to concern himself with care for creation, and requires woman to remain before and help. God determines both the task and relationship of workers.

C. Genesis 2:21–25

"... and He took one of his ribs ... 'This is now bone of my bones ...'"

God made woman from the man so he would know that she is an extension of his own person and nothing foreign—there is no mistake in her nature/creation. Therefore, if a man cares for his wife, he is caring for himself; if she helps, she is helping herself.

"... Therefore a man shall leave his father ... and be joined to his wife ..."

According to creation there is no such thing as an "independent" woman. The man left his family to assume responsibility for another. The woman would remain under the care of her father until a young man *demonstrated* responsibility (see the stories of Ruth, Joseph, and Mary).

"... and they were naked and not ashamed ..."

They were not ashamed because they knew only that God's creation was very good and they were each within the purpose God had given. They had nothing to hide and no one to hide from.

We hide behind excuses when we have rejected God's Word and will for us and when we have expected others to meet our expectations rather than God's purpose.

II. John 8:42–47

". . . You are of your father the devil. . . . He is a liar and the father of it . . ."

A. Genesis 3:1–8

". . . Has God indeed said . . ."

God's Word is the source and substance of all life. The devil attacks that source by leading one to doubt His Word. If I don't believe God has already said something, I choose to believe other words in preference to His, but no other word has life; therefore, I begin to die in that choosing.

". . . nor shall you touch it . . ."

Already, man has fallen. The woman is under attack by the devil's word, and man is not taking responsibility for correcting Eve and rejecting the devil. He has left his purpose knowingly, and death follows. Any time a man rejects his purpose and creator, death follows in his own life and in the lives of all for whom he ought to be responsible (see Romans 5:18 and I Timothy 2:11–15).

"You will not surely die, for God knows . . ."

Every temptation has this thought in common: "God is hiding a better life from you; you could do better if you would choose/act for yourself." Listening to that temptation has and is still killing everyone and every marriage.

"... then the eyes of both were opened ... and they were ashamed."

The knowledge of good and evil did not include the ability to judge rightly nor to choose the good. The choices I make for myself show my inability; God's choices for me demonstrate His goodness and Godhead.

"... and made coverings for themselves ... and hid ..."

The choice for the word of one other than God/the choice for self against God, is followed by endless other choices for self that only make matters worse. To hide from God is to hide from my life and the life giver. To hide from my spouse is to hide from my purpose and take away what I should have provided.

B. Genesis 3:9–19

"... God called to Adam, 'Where are you?'"

This is a question Adam never had to answer before. If we follow God, He is always with us and no one is lost. If we choose our own way, God is not with us. We walk alone; we are lost and have lost God.

" . . . I was afraid because I was naked, and I hid myself . . ."

Being naked before God brought neither shame nor fear until man rejected God's order of life. Man is the one who is now ashamed and hiding because through his actions/lack of responsibility he had contradicted God's conclusion that His creation was "very good."

" . . . the woman you gave to be with me . . ."

First man tries to hide himself behind fig leaves and among trees. When God exposes man in those hiding places, he tries to shift the shame—man accuses both God and his wife of guilt for his sin.

". . . and the woman said, 'The serpent deceived me . . .'"

Eve follows the example of her husband—nothing is her fault, the serpent is to blame. The one problem that prevents all others from being solved is this hiding from truth and responsibility for one's own sin.

". . . He shall crush your head, and you shall crush His heel . . ."

Before God explains the consequences of man's sin, He provides a promise of forgiveness. The Seed of the woman, Jesus Christ, will re-establish God's authority over man, submission to His order of creation, and forgiveness for what is shameful.

". . . in pain you shall bring forth children . . ."

Read verse 16 carefully.

The two things that woman was created to do in paradise were to bear children and help her husband. Since she was determined not to be content with God's order for paradise, she will have a span of life on earth to face the consequences of her own choice in contradiction to God's will.

Now it will be hard for her to bear children and to submit to her husband. The only thing that will make child bearing and submission bearable (even enjoyable) will be a re-submission to God's Word and choice for her.

". . . Because you have heeded the voice of your wife . . ."

Adam faces consequences for his choice as Eve did. Under God's order, Adam would have gladly cared for wife and creation, and wife and creation would have willingly responded to that care. Now Adam will (and we too) have a constant reminder of the results of his choice. Care for the earth will be HARD work and responsibility for his wife is something he MUST (verse 16) do in the face of rebellion (as he rebelled against God).

C. Genesis 3:20–24

". . . God made tunics of skin and clothed them . . ."

Remember, within God's creation, no one and nothing was required to be sacrificed for life. Now that man is sacrificing others for himself, others must be sacrificed to remedy this. Animals (innocent) are killed to make coverings for Adam and Eve—as the Lamb of God will make the covering that takes away sin, guilt, and shame.

" . . . lest he put out his hand and eat and live forever . . ."

God did not choose to drive man out of the garden to punish man. God makes choices always for man's good. God puts man out so that he will not eat from the tree and live forever—AS HE IS.

4

The Ten Commandments in Marriage
The Model Revisited

IV. The Ten Commandments

Deuteronomy 30:1–20

" . . . I have set before you life and death, blessing and cursing; therefore, choose life, that both you and your descendants may live; that you may love the Lord your God, that you may OBEY His voice, and that you may cling to him, for He is your LIFE . . ."

A. "Thou shalt have no other gods before Me."
Deuteronomy 6:4–12: "Hear O Israel, the Lord your God is One . . ."

Paradise was destroyed when man obeyed the authority and voice of another (his own and the devil's). Paradise is given back both eternally and in this lifetime when man returns to THE ONE GOD and diligently listens to HIS Word.

Ephesians 4:4–16: " . . . one God and Father of all . . ."

Paul re-affirms Moses' word from Deuteronomy and explains that the purpose of the written Word, Church, and ministry is to restore UNITY in the knowledge of God.

Jeremiah 8:8–12: ". . . they have rejected the Word of the Lord, so what wisdom do they have? . . ."

If one God is the authority and His Word is in the lives of man and woman, they will draw closer to God and each other in a close bond. Any other word or authority will only offer opportunity for man/woman to choose for self against God and spouse and create a further separation between God and spouse.

B. *"Thou shalt not take the name of the Lord thy God in vain."*

Philippians 4:4–9: ". . . let your requests be made known . . . if there is any virtue, meditate on these things"

God's command is to call upon His Name (Word) and forsake all others. When we refuse or forget to do this, we suffer needlessly. God's command includes holding His Name (Word) before us to the exclusion of the world and its images (words). When we refuse or forget to do this, we needlessly suffer and also cause suffering in others.

C. *"Remember the Sabbath, to keep it holy . . ."*

Hebrews 3:12—4:16: ". . . since a promise remains of entering His rest, let us fear lest any come short of it."

God's Word grants rest from the demands of the Law. God commands rest, which makes time for His Word. His Word teaches us how to rest (to live under grace instead of law). As often as you remain in the Word, you have rest with God (forgiveness) and with others—you serve because you are pleasing/accepted, not in order to earn acceptance.

D. "Honor your father and mother, that it may be well with thee . . ."

Deuteronomy 7:2–4: ". . . nor shall you make marriages with them . . . for they will turn your sons away from following me." (see also 1 Corinthians 7)

God has given parents the responsibility of raising and keeping their children in the faith. In order for parents to fulfill this service, God has given promises (Proverbs 22:6) and commands to children: "Honor father and mother." Honor for God our Father, for father and mother and for marriage is served when children obtain the consent of their parents for their engagement. Parent's consent ought not to be based on personal feelings, but on protecting faith and marriage, by making sure that the two engaged are of the one true faith.

If an orthodox Christian is already married to someone who is not of the same faith, time must be taken to see if agreement can be reached in the faith and if parental consent can be obtained. If agreement in faith cannot be reached, the marriage may remain if the unbelieving spouse will live peaceably within the marriage. If the unbelieving spouse is making it impossible for the believing spouse to remain faithful to God, faith, and marriage, then he/she is free of that bond.

E. "Thou shalt not kill."

Galatians 3:10–14: ". . . for as many as are of the works of the Law are under a curse . . ."

The most serious form of killing takes place when one person imposes the law upon another without a view toward grace. Marriages are cursed and killed when spouses continually judge the performance of the other, while excusing or ignoring their own failures. Marriages are blessed in a context of grace and forgiveness, where each is trying to give, not get—to meet God's expectations and not to invent their own.

F. "Thou shalt not commit adultery."

Psalm 106:34–38: ". . . they mingled with the Gentiles and learned their works . . . they even sacrificed their sons . . ."

Life for man is bearing responsibility for his wife and children. Life for woman is to help man in the bearing of life while submitting to that responsibility. Responsibility rejects self-indulgence; love rejects the sacrificing of others. When men and women choose to be self-indulgent, children are sacrificed, along with the means and purpose of life.

Malachi 2:13–17: ". . . He seeks godly offspring . . ."

When man indulges his passion with a woman but prevents the possibility of conception, he deals treacherously (Genesis 38:1–10).

God's express purpose for the union of man and woman is godly offspring.

Man's rejection of responsibility for the sake of self-indulgence results in sacrifice of children and women. His irresponsibility and self-indulgence leads to violence, abuse, and divorce.

Romans 13:8–14: ". . . make no provision for the flesh to gratify its desires . . ."

Lives are sacrificed any time arrangements are made to prevent or avoid the consequences of one's actions. Careless words, thoughts, spending habits, sexual behavior, etc. all work against the life of individuals and marriages.

I Thessalonians 4:1–8: ". . . each should know how to possess his own vessel in sanctification and honor, not in passion of lust . . ."

Man was created to bear responsibility for the life and well-being of woman. That means keeping himself chaste and abstaining from passion when a woman would not welcome conception. It also means loving physically with a view toward conception, which is the life and honor of the woman (Song of Solomon 3:5).

On Natural Family Planning Versus Artificial Contraception

There is a natural means for dealing with concerns about conception. This natural means seeks to honor God's wisdom in creation and serve the husband's responsibility to care for his wife according to the gospel.

G. "Thou shalt not steal."

Matthew 6:19–24: " . . . For where your treasure is, there your heart will be also."

A marriage cannot remain when spouses are taking from each other to satisfy themselves. It is not the getting or taking of things that makes for life, but taking CARE OF others. You cannot serve the world's idea of wealth (taking all I want from everyone around me, including God, and returning only as much as I feel comfortable with) and have God's true riches. Only caring for and giving of myself protects what God has given me (marriage) and whom He has given me (spouse, children).

H. "Thou shalt not bear false witness against . . ."

Matthew 12:31–37: " . . . for the mouth speaks what the heart is full of . . ."

The hearts we are born with by human nature are evil above all things and desperately wicked. This heart of mine would always see things so that I am right and everyone else is wrong. I can by my own thinking see my spouse as such a horrible person that a loving marriage is impossible even to suggest (2 Samuel 13:15).

God's Word has provided and continues to provide a new heart (Ezekiel 36). This heart does not seek a way to justify its wrong doing by accusing others. This heart knows that as God has determined to love and think well of me, so I am to love and think well of others. God will expose and avenge if I am being taken advantage of. Everyone is served well if I speak helpful words. These words can only be provided by God.

I. "Thou shalt not covet thy neighbor's house, nor wife . . ."

A. Proverbs 15:16–17: "Better is a little with the fear of the Lord, than great treasure with trouble . . ."

To covet is to want something so much that it changes the way you live your life. Remember the fall of Adam. Paradise was being satisfied/content to take care of God's creation in one place, Eden, and in one person, Eve. Satisfaction/contentment does not come from things we can get, but from taking care of what God gives us.

Luke 12:13–21: ". . . for one's life does not consist in the abundance of things he possesses . . ."

If my life consists of what I get from my spouse, from God, from the world around me, nothing will ever be enough and I will continually cast aside what I have in search of more.

If my life consists in the study and care taking of what God has given me, then I will always have an abundance of life in the care I provide and in observing the good results of that care.

5

The Creed
The Nature of God Related to Marriage

V. The Creed

Acts 17:24–31

". . . He gives to all life, breath, and all things. And He has made from one blood every nation of men . . . so that they should seek the Lord."

> A. "I believe in God the Father Almighty, Maker of heaven and earth . . ."
>
> **Romans 1:16—2:6: ". . . for the wrath of God is revealed against all who suppress the truth . . ."**

God is our Creator. God has created us within a gender and with a personal identity to fulfill His purpose in our lives. Any time we choose to suppress this truth in thought, word, or behavior we will meet God's wrath.

> **". . . therefore, God also gave them up . . ."**
> **(Romans 1:24, 26, 28)**

Not only do we suffer direct consequences for refusing God's order/purpose for our lives, we also run the risk of becoming completely blind to that order. Only when we are given completely to God's Word/order are we safe from being given over to the devil and his order (Romans 1:29–32).

"... or do you despise the riches of His goodness ... not knowing that the goodness of God leads you to repentance?"

God is neither good to us nor patient so that we might assume He is pleased with our behavior that is contrary to His created order. He is good in order that we might remember how well He cares for us, even when we care so poorly for one another and ourselves. Repentance would lead us to conform our lives to His order so that we might be a part of His goodness, rather than those who oppose it.

B. "And in Jesus Christ, His only Son, our Lord . . ."

Philippians 3:7–21: "... but indeed I also count all things loss for the excellence of the knowledge of Christ Jesus my Lord, ... that I may gain Christ ... and be found in Him ... that I may know Him ..."

Ephesians 5:22–33 (Read verses 1–21 for fuller appreciation): "Wives, submit to your own husbands, as to the Lord ..."

Wives are to submit to their husbands because life depends on submission to God's order. Wives are able to submit by faith in God, who will always husband them perfectly.

Submitting to husband as to the Lord also includes obeying God rather than men (Acts 5:29) and testing the spirits to see if they are of God (Acts 17:11, I John 4:1).

Wives are commanded to submit to their husbands as Christians are to Christ, because the husband bears responsibility for the life and well-being of his wife.

"Husbands, love your wives, as Christ loved the Church and gave Himself for it . . ."

We are powerless to live before or love God unless He loves us first (He made us alive when we were dead and enemies of His: Romans 5:10, Ephesians 1). So also a woman is unable, even unwilling to submit until she is loved by her husband; that is why his love for her cannot depend in any way upon her response/behavior.

It is love/sacrifice of the husband that allows for the proper behavior of the wife, not the demand of the husband for submission; the Law always kills.

" . . . that He might present it to Himself a glorious church . . ."

We are the primary focus of God's loving attention. God makes all things serve our well-being. Because He loves us, He bears the responsibility of presenting us to Himself in a splendid and holy manner. When we are so presented, we are HIS glory because we are His workmanship (see I Corinthians 1:18–30). Thus, a husband's honor does not come from how he makes himself look in comparison to his wife or in the company of his peers. Rather, his glory is in how well he presents his wife, by taking good care of her spiritually and physically.

When a husband hates his wife (sacrifices her instead of himself), he is ultimately the one who suffers for it in eternity and also in this life—in a cursed relationship.

C. "I believe in the Holy Ghost . . ."

John 14:26–27 and 16:14–15: ". . . but the Helper, the Holy Spirit will . . . bring to your remembrance all things that I said to you. He will glorify Me, for He will take of what is mine and declare it to you."

Romans 10:1–17: ". . . faith comes by hearing, and hearing by the Word of God."

Anyone can bring ruin to his own life by deceiving himself concerning faith. To tell myself I am acting faithfully when I am not puts me in peril of hell and does harm to everyone around me. True faith, godly faith, requires five things:

1. KNOWLEDGE—You cannot believe what you know nothing about.
2. ASSENT—To know it is true; there is no benefit in believing falsehood.
3. OBEDIENCE—Faith means dependence; faith orders behavior and thinking. (e.g.—I believe in gravity; it affects me constantly and I order my life accordingly.)
4. MEMORY—I cannot believe what I cannot remember.
5. ARTICULATION—I cannot obey or act upon what is unclear. Obedience and assurance (comfort) require clear expression in word and thought.

Faith tells me I can love/submit to my spouse without fear, because God is able to restore what may be sacrificed and forgive what I may fail to do.

Faith tells me how to love/submit by holding before me God's explicit Word, which reveals His order in creation.

Faith moves me to do gladly what God desires by the very Word that describes His will.

At this point, we have covered one-third of the Small Catechism as it concerns marriage but have used two-thirds of the pages of this book. From this point on, the material moves much more quickly. The reason is twofold. First, the Commandments and the Creed contain the watershed of divine revelation. The Commandments tell us what is expected of us and the Creed tells us what is provided for us. Upon that foundation we consider the related gifts of God: Prayer, Baptism, the Lord's Supper, and the Keys.

6

The Lord's Prayer
Petitions for an Eternal Union

VI. The Lord's Prayer

Matthew 7:7–12

"*. . . Ask and it will be given to you . . . If you then, who are evil, know how to give good things to your children, how much more will your Father in heaven give good things to those who ask Him!*"

A. "Our Father who art in heaven . . ."

Hebrews 12:1–4: ". . . Looking to Jesus, the author and finisher of our faith . . ."

The order of creation sets the race before us: men, to be responsible for and take care of women and children, women to be faithful helpers of their husbands. This race can only be won by laying aside the burdens the world would impose on us (busyness, commitments, distractions) and the sin that so easily ensnares.

Looking steadily at Jesus gives us both the path to follow and the will/means to follow that path. Image must always be sacrificed for the sake of affecting a good (joyous) reality. Happiness in marriage does not come from being treated the way I thought I should be, but by serving as God intended me to.

If I compare what I think I am suffering wrongfully in my marriage with Jesus, who endured such hostility from sinners, I find that I have really neither served nor suffered, but have only felt sorry for myself.

Hebrews 12:5–11: ". . . shall we not much more readily be in subjection to the Father of Spirits and live? . . ."

The "OUR" in our Father reminds us that we have a common almighty, ever-present Father who works righteously to correct everyone. I may appeal to this Father to help correct my spouse. I accept this Father's correction of me.

If I accept the chastening of the Lord, then I view my spouse and our difficulties as instruction—what there is to be learned from the difficulty (repenting of causes, practicing solutions) and what God is providing for me in my spouse (training in righteousness).

Hebrews 12:12–17: ". . . and make straight paths for your feet . . ."

It is a grave temptation to trade the long-term training of God for short-term remedies that are comfortable or easy. If we reject God's Word and discipline, then we reject Him as our Father and lose every blessing that we might have known.

We are back to looking diligently toward God for counsel and strength. He shows us the straight path to follow. He strengthens us and teaches us to work toward healing. He gives us a mind that rejects bitterness, because bitterness contributes nothing to our well-being or our marriage.

B. "Hallowed be Thy name . . ."

God's name is profaned if we submit to or make sacrifices to any other authority, not only because we have rejected Him as our head, but because this rejection will surely be seen in our marriage. Both our conduct before God and with our spouse will be a disgrace and denial of truth to all who witness it.

In order for God's name (Word) to be our life, all other names (gods/words/authorities) must be rejected.

C. "Thy Kingdom come . . ."

Matthew 13:44–46: ". . . the kingdom of heaven is like a merchant seeking beautiful pearls, who, when he had found one pearl of great price, went and sold all that he had and bought it . . ."

God's kingdom/paradise, comes to us whenever His Word and Spirit are present. God brings His kingdom/paradise into marriage when the husband sees his first responsibility as keeping his spouse (and children) in the Word and when the wife (and children) know that their chief responsibility is to hear the Word. God's Word is that pearl of great price for which we gladly give up all else. That Word at work in the lives of our spouse and children allow them to be always more valuable and more valued in our sight.

Matthew 13:47–52: ". . . therefore every scribe instructed in the kingdom of heaven is like a householder who brings out of his treasure things old and new . . ."

Remaining in the Word will keep us mindful of the treasures God has given us in creation: our image, worth, purpose, etc. Our first and elementary lessons in the Word remain the foundation of faith and life. Daily reading continually grants a fuller understanding, greater appreciation, and a more detailed application—something new to live by and share with our spouse. Daily reading is essential for God's kingdom to be present in marriage.

D. "Thy will be done . . ."
Matthew 19:1–6: ". . . Therefore what God has joined together, let not man separate."

It is just as important to determine if God has joined a man and woman as it is to keep them from separating if God indeed has joined them.

The issue for the Pharisees was finding a reason or how small a reason to make divorce permissible. The issue for Jesus is finding FIRST all the reasons for avoiding one. Our approach to marriage should always be the same as Jesus'.

Ezekiel 18:25–32: ". . . Repent and turn from all your transgressions, so that iniquity will not be your ruin . . ."

When my marriage is having a problem, I tend to compare my spouse's present fault with the whole history of my splendid performance. Even if I have done right in the past, I may have fallen from that righteousness and caused the problem myself. I can undo years of love with a few selfish actions. There is no benefit in comparing my actions (past and present) with my spouse's.

God's will is that we compare our actions with His. Seeing His works and will in the Word shows us what needs to be repented of in our lives, so that we may turn and iniquity may not be our ruin. Iniquity is the ruin of every life and marriage. Repentance and grace from God are the only salvation and life of every person and marriage.

E. "Give us this day our daily bread . . ."

John 6:25–29: ". . . Stop laboring for the food that perishes; rather keep laboring for the food which endures to eternal life, which the Son of Man will give you . . ."

Most people seek a spouse like these people sought Christ, not because they found someone to love (give life for) and serve, but because they found someone to make life easier for them.

The request to God for daily bread is first of all for God to give me strength (food) to give my life on behalf of others. It is not for God to give me whatever I want at this moment, like a spoiled child demands any whim from his parents.

John 6:47–51: ". . . I am the bread of life. . . . Your fathers ate manna in the wilderness and are dead. . . ."

God has already stated that we are not to worry about physical needs since He provides them all without our asking (Matthew 6). What we are to seek is His wisdom/ Word, which gives us life. Israel had miraculous bread in the wilderness, but it could not make them live because they rejected God's Word, promise, and Promised Land (Hebrews 4). If marriage is to live and be a "promised land," it can only do so when we are fed continually with the Word of God.

F. "And forgive us our trespasses as we forgive . . ."

Matthew 7:1–5: ". . . first take the log out of your own eye, then you will be able to see clearly to take the speck out of your brother's."

Here Jesus instructs to judge not, meaning do not condemn a person to hell, because that is God's judgment alone to make. This does not mean we are not to judge one another—meaning we contend for what is right and renounce what is wrong, for the good of one another (James 5:19–20).

Jesus goes on to establish this meaning. He does not forbid us to remove specks from the eyes of others. Rather, He tells us to correct ourselves first.

G. "And may You not bear us along into temptation . . ."
James 1:12–22: ". . . But each one is tempted when he is drawn away and enticed by his own desires. . . ."

This is the only petition of the Lord's Prayer that is not imperative—meaning a command. There is no need to ask God imperatively to NOT lead us into temptation since He never does that. What we are saying in this petition follows: "May the Lord not bear us along into temptation." It means we recognize God as the One who gives us life, breath, and all things. Life has become so easy for us that we forget God's activity and purpose for us (His desires). Therefore, we often eagerly pursue our OWN DESIRES, which ultimately are those of the world and devil. These desires all end in the destruction of our life and our relationship with others. We pray then in this petition that God would not keep life so easy that we run unhindered away from Him and into the world, e.g. God tripped me so I fell before I ran off the edge of the cliff. This petition then asks God to keep reminding me through the circumstances of my life to pay attention to His purpose instead of mine.

1 Corinthians 10:1–13: "... but with every temptation He will provide THE means of escape ..."

The emphasis here must be on THE. God provides the one and only real means of escape from temptation—HIS WORD (see Matthew 4). While God is answering my prayer by pressing me down in my physical life, I may not know or remember how to understand that or endure. God's Word before me daily offers two means of help. First, His Word in my life daily decreases my need for big lessons (physical circumstances) because I am present before His Word to learn a little one daily. Second, His Word teaches me to understand/remember that everything hard for my human nature is good, because it keeps it weak and dependent. Everything hard for my human nature is good for my divine nature because it encourages my love for God's promises and hope of heaven.

H. "But deliver us from the evil one ..."

1 Kings 18:20–22: "... and Elijah came to all the people and said, 'How long will you falter between two opinions? ...' But the people answered him not a word. ..."

If you compare your life and your spouse's with the Bible's teaching on marriage, and identify all the things that are wrong (evil) from which God would deliver you, you still have this question to answer —Do you want to be delivered??? Our flesh has its own desires that war against what is right (our spirit—Galatians 5), and these desires are what make trouble for us/bring death into our lives and relationships. How can God deliver us if we prefer to keep faltering between obedience to Him and ourselves? There is no reason to pray this petition if we don't sincerely want what it asks. If we submit this petition to God without reservations, God will surely answer it and set His Word in our midst to lead us in that deliverance.

Romans 7:14–25: ". . . for I know that in me (that is, in my flesh) dwells no good thing. I find this to be a rule, when I want to do good, evil lies close at hand. . . ."

It is important to remember that this petition concentrates first on the evil in me, my flesh, not in feeling sorry for myself as if I were suffering innocently at the hands of others.

It is important to remember that my flesh is always with me and always instinctively does wrong. If this is to change for the good of my life and relationships, then God's Word must be equally present ("If you remain in My Word you will know the truth, and the truth will make you free" John 8:31).

It is important to remember that once God has delivered me from proud, selfish, and evil thinking to know what is right to do, evil lies close at hand to keep me from doing well. After knowing what to do, I need to be ready for opposition to doing the right thing, and persevere through those temptations.

7

Baptism
Confidence in the Potential of Your Spouse

VII. Baptism

A. What Is Baptism?
Matthew 28:18–20

> **"All authority in Heaven and Earth has been given to Me, therefore, as you go about make disciples of all nations baptizing them . . . teaching them . . ."**

Our Baptism confirms that we have been regenerated in the image of God's Son. We have been anointed in our baptism as Christ (the "anointed One") was anointed in His. Therefore the purpose of our life is NOT to prove that we can get one for ourselves but to give the one we have to others.

B. What Does Baptism Give or Profit?
Mark 16:16

> **"He that believeth and is baptized shall be saved but he that believeth not shall be condemned"**

Baptism provides confirmation of an invulnerable life that is eternal and oriented toward God's will. However, this life exists within a contrary human nature. Our consciousness of these two natures will determine whether we are problem solvers or problem magnifiers.

C. How Can Water Do Such Great Things?

Titus 3:4–8

> " . . . but when the kindness and the love of God our Savior toward men appeared, not by works of righteousness which we have done, but according to His mercy He saved us through the washing of regeneration. . . ."

Water exists and holds the properties it does because the Word of God created it so. Water is perhaps the most compelling witness of nature to the necessity of God's Word and to the properties of that Word to save. Thinking we can have a marriage without the consistent presence of God's Word is like thinking we can live without water.

D. What Does Baptism Signify?

The significance of Baptism, like that of a wedding, is not meant to be frozen in time. Unless the significance of baptism and our marriage moves forward with us we will lose the image and benefits of both.

1. Romans 6:1–11: " . . . likewise you also, reckon yourselves to be dead indeed to sin, but alive to God in Christ Jesus our Lord . . ."

If we fail to distinguish between our human nature and our regenerate soul and the desires of each we are going to ruin our relationships by fighting the wrong battles.

2. Romans 6:12–23: *". . . what fruit did you have then of the things of which you are now ashamed?"*

Jesus said a bad tree cannot bear good fruit (Matthew 15–20). Many marriages are broken or breaking because one person expected or hoped the other would change and become what he/she had hoped for. Change is possible, but good, genuine change can only come by God's grace at work through His Word. If a person is unwilling to give that Word first place in his/her life, what can be expected? There is no good fruit where God's Word is not actively at work. There is no good fruit of expecting a spouse to change himself/herself.

8

The Lord's Supper
Weekly Restoration of Confidence

VIII. LORD'S SUPPER

A. What is the Sacrament of the Altar?

The Sacrament of the Altar is a matter of realizing unions that exist. On the day of the Son, at the rising of the sun, the body of Christ (believers) becomes visible to receive the body and blood of Christ in visible form from the body of Christ in the visible form of the pastor. The Lord's Supper is a feast that celebrates the union between Christ and His bride, the church.

B. What is the Benefit of Such Eating and Drinking?

Wine and bread are physical mediums by which God provides energy to our physical body. The body and blood of Jesus, like His Word, are physical means by which God provides energy for our whole life. God gave us bodies as a means of demonstrating love by providing for the lives of each other.

EXODUS 13:7–10

" . . . unleavened bread shall be eaten seven days . . . It shall be as a sign to you on your hand, and as a memorial between your eyes, that the Lord's Law may be in your mouth; for with a strong hand the Lord brought you out of Egypt."

Egypt meant slavery for Israel. Sin is slavery for us. Our own sin is what keeps us in bondage to all of the ways of thinking, speaking, and behaving which ruin our lives. As God delivered Israel from bondage through the Red Sea, so also God has delivered us from bondage to sin through our Baptism. Now He gives us a testament to keep us mindful of how essential and precious our freedom from bondage is. The Lord's Supper reminds us of our need to be rescued. By the grace of God that rescue is accomplished. The Lord's Supper brings that very rescue into our life and relationships by bringing to us the very body and blood of God that saves us.

C. How Can Bodily Eating and Drinking Do Such Great Things?

The significance of creation is as an extension of God which bears witness to Him. Life could have been some ethereal, immaterial existence and God could create every human out of dust. But God created a physical world by which we might know Him more fully and made us instruments of His creative activity. Physical and spiritual properties do the things they do because God's Word established them so.

D. Who Receives Such Sacrament Worthily?
I Corinthians 10:1—11:34

" . . . but I want you to know that the head of every man is Christ, the head of women is man."

In these two chapters of Corinthians Paul deals with worship, marriage, and the Lord's Supper. Paul's treatment of the three is interwoven because all three have the issue of union at the heart. Worship considers how we unite with God, marriage how we unite to each other, and the Lord's Supper how God unites with us. God and His Word, the Word and elements, the Word and believers—all these unions are made apparent and are celebrated in this feast.

9

Confession and Absolution
The Two Vital Signs of a Relationship

IX. Office of Keys and Confession

A. What is the Office of the Keys?
John 20:22–23

"The Lord Jesus breathed on His disciples and said, 'Receive the Holy Spirit. Whoever sins you forgive, they have been forgiven . . .'"

As Christians, anointed in the image of our savior, we are stewards of His grace. We are called by God to confirm His forgiveness, not decide whether we feel like extending it or not. We forgive on behalf of God, not on behalf or ourselves for we too live under and depend on the mercies of God.

B. What is Confession?

I John 1:8–10

" . . . if we say we have no sin we deceive ourselves and the truth is not in us . . ."

If the time we spend reading God's Word is the pulse of our life and marriage, then the time we spend confessing to and absolving each other is our blood pressure. If we are not confessing it is not because there is nothing to confess (Romans 7); rather we are deceiving ourselves in order to protect our pride. If we deceive ourselves and avoid confession then we are hiding from the truth and it is not long before everything wrong is someone else's fault—especially our spouse's. Remember Genesis 3.

Confession allows my spouse and me (and others) to live in the truth, not hiding anything myself, and not blaming others for what is my fault. Truth allows for mercy (Proverbs 3) and mercy presents no pressure. Mercy presents God's love and care to help, lifting up instead of bearing down upon.

C. What sins should we confess?

Matthew 18:1–35

" . . . moreover if your brother sins go and tell him his fault between you and him alone. If he hears you, you have gained your brother."

Two wrongs don't make a right. God established the process for us to follow to keep one person's wrongdoing from moving others to do wrong. My spouse's faults do not give me the right to condemn nor reject nor be abusive etc. If I think something is wrong, I may inquire—ask for explanations and give time for understanding. If there is something wrong, I may bear witness to it with a view toward reconciliation (Leviticus 19:17). If I get nowhere, I may seek help from others and the Church. Small problems or large makes no difference; God has given us counsel and a Church to keep one person's trouble from becoming everyone's.

D. Which are these?
Colossians 3:12–17

" . . . and forgiving one another, if anyone has a complaint against another, even as Christ forgave you . . . But above all these things put on love, which is the bond of perfection . . ."

Notice that the Bible does not command us to "TRUST" one another. It does tell us to LOVE—the love that sacrifices self for others. Why should we put our trust in other people or expect them to be trustworthy when we by nature are not? Why should we expect of others what we cannot render to them or God? So we love one another and our spouse in particular because this alone—this love created and sustained by God's Word—gives us what is required for a permanent relationship.

10

Concluding Remarks
How to Keep This Mindset in the Mix

X. Conclusion

Philippians 3:1–2a

"*. . . for me to write the same things to you is not tedious, but for you it is safe. Beware . . .*"

Man's purpose is to be responsible, loving, and the caretaker of God's creation. The root of all his sin is to avoid this.

Woman's purpose is to remain before and help her husband. The root of a woman's contradiction to God's design lies in her determination to overrule this order.

All people are deceived by Satan with the thought that both happiness and unhappiness come from the people and things around me. The source of my unhappiness is, in fact, the disorientation of my will. Real happiness comes from the power of God's Word to regenerate, reorient, and provide for my life.